REFLECTIONS OF THE TAO – FORWARD

Here's a collection of poems I decided to write in early 2018 and completed in late 2020. The premise of the book was to write a poem for each verse of the Tao Te Ching, to reflect its wisdom through my own experience of life and my own understanding of that wisdom which is contained in this ancient book.

It is not meant as an exposition of its contents, just my own reflections on its essential ideas. The Tao Te Ching is a book of wisdom that has been handed down for well over two millennia and was written by Lao Tzu.

I hope this collection of poems will either introduce you to the Tao or reacquaint you with it. I believe its insights into life are much needed today by each one of us.

You can download a copy of an English translation of the original book here: https://shorturl.at/zT039 (or alternatively if you have a smart phone use the QR Code at the end of the Index).

The first verse of the Tao reads "The Tao that can be told is not the eternal Tao". So, I do not claim that by reading my book you will have gained its wisdom, just my reflections of it.

In effect my book is not the Moon, it is a finger pointing at the Moon. I hope you will make your own study of the book and maybe share your insights with me and with others.

The Tao Te Ching provides us with a deep understanding of the nature of reality and the universe itself and is also known as "The Book of the Way and Its Virtue".

Each time one of my poems mentions THE TAO or THE WAY I have capitalised these words to draw the reader's attention to the concept about which this poetry is written.

I have also used a capital when mentioning Source, it is my word for what others may call God, Source Energy, Life, etc. I found my own reflections on The Tao, to be both enlightening and inspirational for me and so in that way it has already fulfilled its purpose. I do however hope that it will be enlightening for you too.

I was raised as a Christian and was at one time a lay preacher in the Methodist Church and wonder if Jesus read the Tao, because I hear echoes of the Tao in his words. Now, I am neither a Taoist nor a Buddhist, but I am a wisdom seeker.

Wisdom is wisdom from wherever it arrives, and the fact that the Tao Te Ching has survived and has been revered for so long, tells you much about the value of its content.

Please treat my book as a gateway into new thoughts and understandings of an ancient wisdom that I believe has great relevance to all our lives today. Thank you so much for buying your copy.

Barnabas England - 28th March 2024

REFLECTIONS ON THE TAO - INDEX

Here's a QR Code to enable you to download a pdf copy of an English translation of the Tao Te Ching

INTRODUCTION - IN PRAISE OF THE TAO

There is a way that seems right
Whose end is in destruction
Those whose eyes are not wise
Lead to this path's construction

I ask you please, get on your knees
Get grounded in THE TAO
Let its words, end the absurd
In the here and now

Let unseeing eyes, open surprised
To see such wisdom here
Be blessed for all your life
And you will shed less tears

THE TAO TE CHING, real peace will bring
Please take in its delights
Its insights embraced, can set the pace
For a life of love and light

I - FINDING THE PEACE

Let go and let god
Let your desires drift
On the sea of tranquility
As you accept life's gift
Let the mystery unfold
Let it flow through you
Wanting, yet desiring less
Allowing all that's true

Invisibly manifest
Stop defining things
Open minded to uncertainty
Feel the peace it brings
Trust in the life force
That has brought you here
Then all you need to know
Will suddenly be clear

II - ESCAPING DUALITY

In this duality
It seems impossible
To live without judgement
And yet, I may have found a key
To unlock the ups and downs
And to live in serenity
Be one who loves
So that you can see

Ugliness and beauty
Exist side by side
It is only our judgement
That you and I decide
What's acceptable
And if we'll take the ride
Of believing what we're told
Or end the tears we've cried

To live in this up and down world
To see what's wrong and right
To live without judgement
We must synthesise our flight
With left and right wings flapping
And keep the end in sight
When we dissolve into the oneness
And end dualism's plight

So, let the world go by
Let you be you, and me be me
Realise, that to harmonise
What's here will make us free
Accept the unacceptable
With never ending glee
In our shells, escape from here
Transcend this world
And move into eternity

III - UNDISTURBED

Still waters
Be content
Choose to accept what is
Let serenity touch your life
Let calmness be your trademark
And undisturbed you'll be

For as desire strengthens
Forceful you'll become
You'll call attention to your actions
And dark responses you will stir

Accept what you are given
Be grateful for what is yours
And more will be added
Through life's open door

So, be at peace, don't complain
Or put yourself in the firing line
Be blessed, in undisturbedness
Show love and all will be fine

IV - SPACE

In the space between your thoughts
Is silence
In the space between possessions
Lies contentment
In the emptiness of space
The universe is held together
Space, a place of peace

For when we have space
We can breathe
When there is space
All opinions can exist
When we allow space
For disagreement
Enemies can become
Best friends

The nothing that wisdom says I am
Provides the space for me to be
Everything through love
In all eternity
All the twisted knots are loosened
Unravelling in the space where we exist

The emptiness is filled
Within the fullness of all space
We are divinity expressed
In the smile of the Father's face
The dust settles
In the infinity of space

V - THE INDIVISIBLE INVISIBLE

The sun shines on the righteous
And on the wicked too
Its provision does not discriminate
In THE WAY of me and you
Breath is given to the good
But evil men can breathe
So, will you side with duality
Or in oneness, will you find peace

Let not judgement of those different
To you ... make you feel sad
Instead accept we are all
Individuals ... and be glad
The one whose path's a journey
You would never take
Has a right to be themselves
Though you say, it's a mistake

Find harmony and peace
Relax and allow all that is
Try to understand
But if you can't, then enter bliss
Remember that one day the Mountains
Will be lost into the sea
And the crooked places will be
Straightened, and we'll all be free

Your view of life has the same value
As anyone that you meet
So, don't sound the alarm
And you won't need to retreat
Ask for guidance, be fair-minded
Lose the need to create waves
And then the ten thousand things
Won't trouble you, as you give them space

VI - THE ROOT OF CREATION

The energy that brought us here
The spark of me and you
The vivacity of eternal spirit
Fills the universe right through
As co-creators now
With divine vibrancy
The root of creation
Flows through you and me

Inherent creativity
Is what we all possess
So, bring to birth new ideas
Let Maya be impressed
That the illusion that she brings
Can be changed to fit our will
That the dream reality
Isn't run of the mill

As a child of the universe
Glide high upon her wings
Soar up to the heights
Transcend anger, fear, such things
Be the presence holy
Rising up to play your part
Ride THE TAO of existence
Live it from your heart

Being separate from love
Is the hardest thing to do
So, reunite with spirit
And create, make all things new
You were sent here to
Enhance, exalt, increase, intensify
To raise this world's vibration
To unfold your gifts, not to die

VII - BE A WITNESS TO LIFE

Are you striving not arriving
Do you never feel complete
Have you noticed that nature
Gives willingly, without defeat
That the selflessness of what is
Can never be out-given
That THE WAY to have all things
Is to act like you're in heaven

Earth and heaven endures eternal
Because they exist for you
Not for themselves do they take
But give, is all they do
So, the wise chose to witness life
To serve, and to observe not grasp
That is why they flourish
And they themselves will last

So, stop the chase, and be a witness
Be a giver, let your desires go
Let life come to you
End the misery and the woe
Of trying to chase the wind
And in contentment be
The one who outlives what's passing
And you'll share eternity

VIII - IN HARMONY WITH WHAT IS

Nature flows, it's how to be
Like water reaching depths easily
Feeding the roots
Producing fruits
Giving blessings from the I, to the we

We must accept what exists
Working alongside what persists
To hold out is a mistake
We must all be awake
Or our lives will be lost in the mist

Dwell close to the land
Then you'll understand
The weakness of tangents flown high
Go deep into your heart
And then you can start
To fully understand the why

Be gentle and kind
Make up your mind
That close to nature you'll be
In harmony with what is
You'll enter bliss
Then what to do, you'll see

IX - THE WAY OF HEAVEN

When is full too full
What makes your senses dull
More is less they say
So, find a better way
Enough for the world’s need
But not for the whole world’s greed

Too much, makes you sick
Contentment is the trick
Know your limit, rest awhile
It's sure to make you smile
THE WAY of heaven’s call
Is happiness for all

Be humble, watch your step
That’s the way to be blessed
Don't lose your edge
Don't be jaded or a wretch
Too much gold will weigh you down
No more smiles only frowns

X - PLAYING THE FEMININE PART

Leadership that doesn't dominate
No need to seek control
Governing without self importance
With lots of heart and soul
Loving those you lead
Giving birth to hope
Avoiding separation and
Helping others cope

Hold onto, oh so lightly
The favours of this life
Be grateful not demanding
Don't grasp, and you'll avoid strife
Work without seeking credit
Find delight in what you give
See it in the smiles on others faces
And you'll have learned how to live

By living in both soul and body
Paradoxes will fall away
When the world is seen in balance
Absolutes, like night and day
Disappear into the middle
Of the existence of all things
And equipoise returns
And all its blessings brings

XI - THE VOID

Emptiness goes unnoticed, but
Usefulness depends on what is not
Like walls create a room
The void at the centre of our lives
Is what gives life meaning

The space between the notes
Makes the tune
The cacophony of noise
That would ensue
Ends in beauty and in silence
The void is where meaning exists
Without silence, there is no music

It's the life force that creates the tree
Not trunk, branches, or leaves
Without this invisible empty force
There is but wood and compost
The void is life, it's invisible

The vital essence of our lives is
The indivisible, the emptiness, the void
Pay attention to this nothingness
For it is your essence

This no-thing-ness is the real you
You are not flesh, blood and bones
You are life, the eternal spirit
You are the void!

XII - THE CHASE

How do you navigate your life
For you, is it a sensory experience
Do vibrant colours attract you
Do sweet sounds fill your day
Do you look at the creation
Or for the creator

Do you chase the moon
Or do you seek inner peace
Do you have the attitude of gratitude
Or do you always want more
How is this life for you
Do you struggle or do you snuggle

The enlightened one has given up the chase
Contentment is their watchword
They have gone within and found understanding
They know they are in the world but not of it
The ephemeral and its passing illusory beauty
Like all physical forms find its roots in the miraculous

Let your mind be at peace
Conserve your energy
Let your growth as a spiritual being
Be unimpeded by the chase
Allow things to come and go
You are the miracle divine

XIII - YOUR'S IS NO DISGRACE!

See yourself in others
For the divine light rests with all
See beyond form, to the formless
Realise that there's no wall
Between life, within you and without you
The rest is but a dream
For we are fellow travellers
We're all on the same team

The separation, a mere illusion
Trouble and alarm it brings
The universe, is the one song
We all harmonize and sing
Different notes from the same music
An eternal, joyful hymn
All discord a mis-perception
Not making divine light dim

So, remain independent
Of what people say of you
There is no right or wrong
To all you say and do
For we are playing
Our part in the orchestra of life
Each sound that we are making
Doesn't need to end in strife

We can be ourselves, and favour
Is not something to fight for
A cause of alarm that demeans us
That shocks us to the core
Don't degrade yourself by seeking
The approval of the selves that aren't you
Without the self, you'll never pity
And true peace you'll never lose

XIV - INTUITION

Intuition helps us to see,
See, hear, and feel
That which is beyond the senses

Intuition reveals to us
The unknowable
That without beginning or end

Intuition is the sixth sense
By which we understand
Ourselves and our place
In time and space

Through intuition
We can be at peace
Within our own lives

We can understand the oneness
Which is the essence of all things
Intuition reveals us as we are

We can see how things
Have always been
Beyond the world of form
Here the invisible is revealed
... by intuition

XV - AMORPHOUS

Shapeless shapes eternal
Described, as indescribable
Ready to take on the form
Of life itself, so inevitable

Potential of perfection
Indeterminate in design
A silhouette in profile
Not wishing to beguile

The masters of the last age
No cunning, just subtle wisdom
No need to be defined
Vague and yet profound

Alert, watchful, simple
Like hollow caves and melting ice
Amorphous human beings
Beautiful and wise

Like clearing muddy waters
They are not arising into life
Because in stillness they existed
Time passed then they were ripe

XVI - DESTINY'S PERSPECTIVE

Let the world go by
Give distance to your thoughts
See the transient ebb and flow of all things
Do you want peace

Peace comes as you realise
The circle of life is a blessing
Destiny's perspective
Can be found in silence

Empty yourself of all but love
Let things come and go
Find passion in the moment
But don't cling on

Don't cling to the past
For endings are beginnings
And all things to return to Source
Give up your thoughts

There at your roots is peace
The transient will pass
Find peace in the eternal
And live

In steadfastness lies insight
Let the past pass
Let the future unfold
Just be

Be impartial
Let your perspective be
Destiny is peace, it can be trusted
It's what's meant to be

XVII - LEAVING NO TRACE

Be an enabler
Say very little
Don’t let people remember you
Help them find their own abilities
Encourage them to use their talents
And you will be a great leader

Be an observer, be aware of what is
And then gently nudge things along
Delegate responsibility
Leave little or no trace of your ideas
Let people think they prevailed
And you will be a great leader

Stay in the background, don’t interfere
Help create an environment
Where others can take responsibility for their actions
A nod, a smile, a frown
Can be the only thing needed
For your silent love to show THE WAY

XVIII - BEING VIRTUOUS

Our laws ask us to act virtuously
And yet no rules are needed
To be applied to those
Who are being virtuous

Action that arises from the heart
From a sense of belonging
To the whole of humanity
Shows love and kindness to all

Actions based on fear
Of what the law may do to you
May appear virtuous
But is really only hypocrisy

Don't let virtue be an act
Or absent from your heart and life
The absence of virtue in your heart
Will cut you off from abundant life

Live in peace with the oneness
Know you belong to the whole
By seeing yourself in others
You will treat everyone as you

XIX - SIMPLICITY

The law of love transgressed
Written on the human heart
Resulted in a world
That's been flawed from the start
To be wiser than the rest
A saint in other's sight
Ended when the ego rose
And soon began a fight

To be moral and to be just
To know what's right from wrong
Has different opinions released
Resulting in a discordant song
Industry and profit
Lead us all to shame
For money is not love
And it turns life into a game

Outward forms alone
Cap doffing to an ideal
Dotting "I"s and crossing "T"s
Is not a love that's real
Cast off selfishness
End temper's desire
And in simplicity
Rekindle the heart's fire

XX - A GUEST IN THIS WORLD

Light is shining everywhere I look
I see great abundance
I accept gratefully what is given
I am a guest in this world
I am sustained by the great mother

Therefore: I do not live in fear
I do not need to discern the duality
I am free from the cares of others
Drifting, without a place to go
Alone, awaiting my first smile

My mind is simple, unadulterated
I may seem like an ignoramus
And yet; I do not strive
I have no worries
I drift as a wave on the ocean

Staying outside the grooves
Set for me, free of expectation
A guest in this world
Avoiding the limelight
I'm at peace as aimless as the wind

XXI - TOUCHING THE INVISIBLE

Elusive, formless, vague
But giving rise to form
Virtuous are her followers
Who have touched the invisible

THE TAO though obscure and dark
Is the life breath, spirit and essence
Of all the thousand things
That make up the world of shapes

To know the beginning
I need to see within myself
Then I can remember
How the world was formed

Touching the invisible
Seeing without eyes
Hearing the call of spirit
Is what makes us wise

XXII - THROUGH THE STORMS

No goals, no desires, no judgments
No concern for the outcome
Choose to accept what is

Be one who bends, not breaks
Who is empty, so can be filled
Live your life in peace

Flow with the energy of creation
Everything you do will succeed and
Failure will become impossible

Let all opinions stand
Let others be who they are and
As you embrace others, they will embrace you

Bend with the wind, be not broken
And like a giant palm tree you will stand
Through the storms of your life

XXIII - THE WAY OF HEAVEN

In nature you can see a pattern
How long does a strong wind blow
Gentle breezes and stillness follow
Storms are unsustainable
They dissipate
Talk don't shout
Let your silence roar

A downpour of rain doesn't last
The clouds empty
The Earth is replenished
The dryness begins
Whisper don't talk
Let silence be your hallmark

Let your ways be the way of heaven
Let divine power flow through you
Let nature be still
Instead, be strong in THE WAY
Don't let your life force fail
Be one who walks in THE WAY

Let everything fall into place
Trust your inner voice
Listen carefully to it
You were meant to be ...
You are, a child of heaven

XXIV - THE GIFT OF LIFE

Rather than seeing yourself
From the point of view of the ego
As God's gift to the world
Relentlessly promoting yourself and your virtues
Pushing your own conceited agenda
Instead ... live a thankful life!

See where you are in life
In a better place than some for sure
But in a worse place than others
With gratitude accept what you have been given
And life can and will add more

All you possess
Family, friends, health, money
Are all entrusted to you
So be a wise steward
Your talents you must treat the same

See the gift of life turn full circle
Freely you have received
With the attitude of gratitude in your heart,
Become one who gives
Give the gift of life, in abundance

XXV - FORMLESS PERFECTION

Before the worlds began
Before the universe was here
The formless perfection, THE TAO
Brought all into being, it's clear
Solitary, empty, unchanging
Eternal and serene
The beauty of the infinite
Was nowhere to be seen

The mother of us all
The creator and the thought
Behind the emptiness
From which everything was wrought
Boundless greatness beckoned
We on tiptoe were asked to stand
To see all that was emerging
Of what THE TAO had planned

So great the mother was
All that proceeded in nobility
Heaven, Earth, and People
With THE WAY it all should be
So, to understand your importance
In all that now exists
Look at the purpose behind all things
And see the grandame's face

XXVI - CALMNESS COMES

Of the ten thousand things
There are a few that concern me
I have found peace within
About most things in this life

But letting go of these last things
Prove to me, my ego is not yet silent
I know that calmness comes
To those who let go and let God

Why am I left in this quandary
Where I know the peace available
To let go of these last few things
Seems like the end of me

I have always been passionate
An all or nothing type of guy
Can I choose nothing
Before it chooses me
And let calmness come, before I die

XXVII - FOLLOWING THE LIGHT

There's a light that shines
In your heart and mine
It's there to brighten darkness
For ever and all time
Illuminating the path
Of those perceived wrong or right
And it's clear that all of us
Should be following the light

For when the light is followed
We can see the truth
That you are me
And I am you
Without the light shining
We are sleeping in the dark
And we all miss the joy
Of living in the light

So, speak without causing harm
Travel without leaving a trace
Know the unlocked is safe
The untied knot, a saving grace
Abandon no-one
Be an impartial guide
Live your life
Following the light

XXVIII - CONSTANT VIRTUE

Be a valley under heaven
Care is gentleness not strength
Your virtue will not fade
A childlike trust will go to any length

Keep your steps in line with heaven
Whilst on earth you show the way
Do not deviate from the route given
And the infinite path you'll display

Keep humble, but learn splendour
And by eternal power you'll act
Be abundant life's example
Quench the thirst of every lack

Don't lose your spirit's virtue
As you live in the world of form
Be unattached by preserving
The qualities possessed when you were born

Lightly row your boat
Gently down the stream
For as you were told
This life is but a dream

XXIX - AN UNFOLDING LIFE

A vessel of perfection
Yours an unfolding life
Always unerring in direction
With no need to strive

Some days ahead
Some days behind
A time to use your vigour
And a time to rest your mind

Don't always play safe
Sometimes be more keen
But nothing extravagant
Excessive, extreme

Life’s not to grasp
To control or to improve
You’re here to breathe in and out
But mainly to love

Your life is sacred
There’s no need to lose
Just let your life unfold
It is the best way to move

XXX - THE WAY TO WALK

Hearts and minds to win
Put brutish force away
If by the sword you live
By the sword, you'll die one day

Make sure your life and all
Find a good use for its spark
Let your energy flow in kindness
In this way make your mark

To stop the land from being cursed
To make sure the crops don't fail
Put an end to war, stop the fight
Let peace be, in hill and vale

Let not briars and thorns grow up
Take not sides find common ground
Magnanimous if in victory
In your joy, let love be found

Let pride be gone from you
Let boasting be unheard
Kindness in your actions show
And in every spoken word

THE WAY for us to walk
Is in the paths of peace
It's time to be a friend to all
And let every trouble cease

XXXI - VICTORY

Victory is spelt vanquish
There's destruction in its path
A funeral procession caused by ego
A travesty born of wrath

To prevail upon this earth
To love killing is not THE WAY
Decent people love peace and quiet
Hatred with love they pay

Weapons are the tools of evil
And detested by lovers of THE TAO
Arms have only brought sadness
To the here and now

Give up the desire for victory
Let us all forever live in peace
Find a way to show love
So, war and violence cease

XXXII - OM

The mind defines what is
Negates the beauty of a kiss
Makes a tree an object
Instead of letting it just live

Words matter and yet the truth
Explaining puts an end to youth
There's no need to correct
Then nothing turns to dust

Good, you need not specify
There's nothing to decide
End the need for mistakes
All things are sweet and must

End the need for walls
For love trumps over all
Division is what's fake
Let's end decay and rust

Let creation like a river flow
Into the ocean, like rain and snow
Let life's cycle be complete
Let love reign without defeat

XXXIII - A BLESSED LIFE

To understand others is to know
But wisdom is yours
When you understand yourself
With force you can master others
But it takes strength
To master yourself

True riches are yours
When you realise you have enough
And until you do
Life will seem quite tough

For a long life
Accept the place ordained for you
To live forever
Let life, live itself through you

Be a blessing to the world
Be who you're meant to be
Following your calling
Is what will set you free

XXXIV - THE GREAT SCHEME OF THINGS

Life and love are the constants
Of the universe
Like a river they flow through all
Uninterrupted
In the duality
There appears to be a great divide
And yet ...

Ceaselessly
Without dichotomy
The oneness has its way
There is no fight
Both left and right, up and down,
In and out rely
On THE GREAT WAY

THE TAO neither
Commands, controls
Nor takes possession
Of the will of those who follow
The life giving spirit
In each step they take

Greatness is achieved by the wise
In realising that, like the sky
Covers the Earth
Everything returns to its place
No domination is necessary
For us to be who we are
In the great scheme of things

XXXV - THE ONE AND THE WAY

For those who seek peace
Security and happiness
They find it in the oneness

No harm comes to them
Who seek out the those that
Keep themselves true to the one

The pleasures of this Earth
Are but a fleeting treasure
Delicious for a moment, then gone

Bland and insipid these delights
Compared to THE WAY ...
Why even consider such emptiness

There is no sensory evidence
To see, or hear, about THE WAY
Yet, it is inexhaustible and eternal

To give up your days, even your life
In pursuit of the oneness and THE WAY
Is to attune yourself to wisdom

XXXVI - THE WISDOM OF OBSCURITY

The ego is ready to boast
To show the world all it has
So, choose THE WAY of wisdom
And have a peace that will last

If I promise nothing to you
And deliver all that you ask
I've made my work easy for me and
Disappointments I've left in the past

Let what's weak become strong
Let go of what you wish to contain
Let flourish what you would remove
Give access to what you'd restrain

For the gentle outlasts the strong
Weakness revealed is true strength
The wisdom of obscurity
Is something to take to great length

The deep water's fish mustn't leave
Nor a nation show its sway
Concealed and vague be the truth
Until the need for it to be displayed

XXXVII - EFFORTLESS PERFECTION

Let striving cease
Let’s find release
From actions clamoured for
Let's know the peace
And live at ease
Let our spirits soar

In nature there’s a rhythm
A melody so pure
Creation hums the music
The heartbeat of our world
The tune is deep within us
Nothing we must learn
Relax into perfection
And let life’s passion burn

Let pretences fall away
Let all you do and say
Reflect the joy you've found within
Show it's here to stay
That you have found THE WAY
To live but never sin

When calm and silence prevail
You will never fail
The universal anchor in your heart
Will enable you to sail
Surviving winds and gales
Enabling you to play your part

Effortless perfection
By finding the connection
Between all things and you
You'll have such great affection
Whate'er your life's direction
When you find peace that's true

XXXVIII - LIVE OUT YOUR OWN TRUTH

A life of rules and regulations
Has never brought you peace
Following instructions
Surely has to cease
Acceptance of the oneness
Must conclude in this
Living out your own truth
Is the way to bring you bliss

For morality is less than goodness
Ritual is lesser still
It's just a husk of faith
Next is chaos, a bitter pill
So, act without a sense of self
Give without condition
Let justice be without preference
Blind seeing, is no contradiction

The heart is pure, so meditate
Let your actions be from there
Respond to your high calling
No rules can compare
To relying on the sacred self
For trying to be good you'll fail
Live a life of knowing
Be you, and gently sail

XXXIX - PLAYING YOUR PART

To belong to everything
To see yourself as part of the whole
Demands that you each day
Are playing your part

Like birds without the sky
Fish without the sea
A car without an engine
A table without its chairs

Your integrity demands
You are like the breath
Of one who is alive
In and out it goes

Virtue is to be found in the whole
Standing out from the crowd a mistake
Show true humility by
Living in accordance with creation

Be humble, have honour
But not too much
Shining too brightly
Robs yourself of your rightful place

XL - YIELD!

Let go and let God
Humility, acceptance, peace
As we live and breathe
As our motions are set on course
By a power greater than ourselves
By the One who lives within
Yield!

There is a wisdom here
To play our part in life
We need to listen to the heart
The higher self
And in the passions of the day
To be aware of our place
In the great scheme of things and
Yield!

XLI - UNSOPHISTICATED

All things are but perception
What can make you smile
Could be ultimate wisdom
If you look back in a while

It is the scorn and ridicule
Which those with laughter make
That others realise is sweetness
And joy without mistake

To see in darkness
What others cannot see
To appear to go backwards
When advancing is not retreat

To appear tarnished, but yet pure
To take the easy way is hard
To have true power may seem weak
Whilst not holding the right cards

What seems indifference to some
Is true love in a place of peace
The unsophisticated
Is true art in a neophyte's dream

A childlike wisdom you should crave
Hidden from those in so called maturity
To have fulfilment in this life
You must ponder eternity

XLII - COMBINATION AND COMPROMISE

There is but one in essence
But in duality we abide
Within this reality
We're always keep taking sides

Our opinions matter
Diversity brings forth
A multi-hued experience
Of east, west, south and north

A boring place this world would be
If we all were the same
But in synthesis and concession
Our egos can be tamed

The ten thousand things exist
In perfect harmony
When we all take the time
The others point to see

For if we believe too fervently
In having our own way
The power of combination and
Compromise will end today

It can be seen that losing
Ends in a greater gain
And those who win their way
In that win cannot remain

XLIII - NON-ACTION

The hand in the glove
A hardness made soft
An empty void
Nothing, easily fills
In a similar way
Achievement
Arrives without effort

In quietness, learn
To convey your intentions
Without movement
Not many understand this
But the wise do
That is why not many
Receive this worlds riches

Live softly
Seek wisdom within
And life will become easy for you

XLIV - LOSING YOURSELF

A reputation and possessions
May cost you, yourself
A price much too high to pay
The trouble you gain in the end isn't worth it
Don't seek this worlds wealth, I say

The sweet fragrance
Of a crushed flower
Will lovingly scent any place
Love's a sacrificial fruit
True wealth a kind gift
Which has no bitter taste

Contentment in good times and bad
Gives you a lifetime
Without disappointment
Knowing when to stop
Preserves you from peril
Endurance is the life of a saint

XLV - APPEARANCES

Appearances can be deceiving
All is not as it seems
Face value is not the best view
Of the depths to this world or our dreams

The universal constant is
Stillness and tranquillity
We were sent here to act
But our observations give us clarity

In this temporal reality
One day our voices will be silent
Life will go on without us here, so
Make sure your life is wisely spent

First glance may be lasting
In our memories and yet
A wiser man will think of
All the times with which he's met

So, let fullness be as empty
As intelligence, stupid be
Let activity conquer the cold
As inactivity conquers heat

XLVI - THE BLISS OF ETERNITY

Free will, the choice is yours
Resources to use at your peril
To create or to tear down
Make a better world or go to war

Wanting what isn't yours or
Being thankful for your blessings
If you're looking for bliss
Be a follower of THE WAY

To reject contentment is foolish
To embrace the way of destruction
Will not help you find
The bliss of eternity

XLVII - ACTIONLESS ENLIGHTENMENT

The heart keeps beating
It is at work
Calling you to trust
In your inner wisdom
Which is always there

There's no information to collect
When in spirit you be
Without moving
You can know
All there is to be known

You are connected to the whole
Use your inner eyes to see
Be at peace with what is
Find THE WAY
In the rhythm of your heart

Be complete
Where you are now
Don't chase the moon
The learning you seek
Is waiting here for you

XLVIII - LETTING THINGS GO

The wisdom of the ages
Is to let the river flow
Don't fight the tide
Accept what is
Let what matters to you
Go where it will go

Don't fret, don't be fearful
Walk in faith and love
Believe that there’s a plan
Accept the smooth with the rough

Interfering creates drama
Your sadness won't diminish
The more you kick against the goads
Your heartache will never finish

Learning accumulates knowledge
But knowledge weighs you down
Decreasing your actions into nothing
Will give you smiles instead of frowns

XLIX - GOOD, KIND AND FAITHFUL

There are those who we find to be
Good, kind, and faithful to us
It is easy to be that way with them
But to do good to those
Who don't is hard
But I promise you, it can be done

To be good, kind and faithful
To those who are bad, unkind
And unfaithful
All you must remember
Is to see other people
As if they were you

Treat everyone as your own child
Live in harmony with all
Love them from your heart
And then, your childlike ways
Will draw others to you
They will all want to be your friend

L - THE DEATH OF DEATH

Immortal! Born again!
Passed from death to life
The concept of an end
Itself shadowed in love and light

The death of death is here
In these words of mine
Stop following after life, or death
Or journeying between them in a line

Contemplate yourself as a being
Outside time and space
An eternal one who is much more
Than a part of the human race

Don't cling to this passing world
Don't clutch to this life oh so frail
Its transient ways may beguile us
It is wanting us to fail

Let your spirit dwell in the place
Wherein death cannot be
When you know your truest essence
From death you will be free

Nothing can touch the soul
Of one who no longer fears
Beasts, weapons other men
Here is the end to tears

LI - HIDDEN VIRTUE

Springing into existence
Life emerges from source
Individuality beckoned
This life wasn't forced

Springing forth soul unconscious
As perfect as it's free
Was how all of us began
Including you and me

Unfolding into existence
To be completed is THE WAY
Valuing Source's treasures
With each passing day

Worship not commanded
But spontaneously as if by design
THE WAY is always followed
As a leader so benign

It's hidden virtue nourished
From the cradle to the grave
Source produced didn't possess
All the life it gave

LII - THE PRACTICE OF ETERNAL LIGHT

From the mother all life emerges
Great and small
Life itself was given to each one
And in that life is the light

Not the light of a thousand stars
But the light of the thousand things
The mother is the source of the light
The light of life

All that exists has its origin in her
We are a family of light
Gaia, people, animals
Reptiles, birds, fish and insects

Our Source is where we will return
In silence we learn the wisdom
Of our connectedness
So, be in awe of who we are ...

And that we all belong
Together, in her
The great mother
The source of light and life

LIII - A LITTLE SENSE

Kindness and compassion
Will remove distressing disguises
Guilt is not required
When following the great way
Amassing great wealth
Living in opulence
Only hurts the balance
Of the oneness to which you belong

All of nature has no problem
In playing out its part
In living out its purpose
Only human beings get a choice
Of being kind and helpful
As a wilful act and yet
Many choose instead
Just to feather their own nests

With just a little sense
Turn your curse into a bless
When you see the less fortunate
It's your time to help
Enough for all our needs
But not for the greed
Of the ones taking paths
That lead them astray

It easy to see why
There are those who die
When there is no mercy to be found
Those left in poverty
Are just as you and me
While the rich man
Sat in the trappings of great wealth
Eats his fill until he's sick

LIV - THE MICROCOSM AND THE MACROCOSM

A bird's eye view
From a distance
Way back in space-time
All is one
Everything belongs together
Dichotomies end
It all makes sense

Close up
In the duality
Things seem separated
As if there are differences
Sides to belong to
And yet we all are one
So, find reasons to belong
To the whole

In prayer and meditation
As we look within
We can remember
That life is one
And those who would separate us
Have only fear to offer
And love to banish

LV - HARMONY'S CHILD

Like a newborn infant
On arrival here
So pure, so heavenly
With nothing to fear

You are whole
Nothing troubles you
In union with all
No need to feel blue

To grow and to wither
Is not your life's plan
But to know love eternal
And to really understand

You're harmony's child
Changeless, unique
Transcending duality
In oneness complete

LVI - THE SECRET EMBRACE

To reach the unreachable
To commune with the divine
You need to silence your voice
You must ignore the mere sensory
And enter the primal

Go beyond the cares of men
The hustle bustle
Don't be attached to anything
Release your desires
And be fully free

When you enter
The highest state of being
You will be in the dearest place
In people's hearts
And you will be embraced
By all that is, that's the secret embrace

LVII - BECOMING YOURSELF

I seek to influence
I want to contribute
I want to help
But wisdom says be silent

I want to plan
To have my energy harnessed
To see a clearer path
But instead I find peace

Power seeks to control
The law has become a burden
Interference creates anger
Let life flow

Enablers stand back and
Let others make their own journey
Let the fog roll in
But see the mists lift

Life is a step by step unfolding
An undoing of what was done
A place of peace and wisdom
For each to become themselves

LVIII - GREAT LEADERSHIP

The leadership we lack
The leadership we need
Is the leadership of example
Not the leadership of greed

Burdens should be lifted
For the imposition of the will
Of a ruler, makes us restless
It shows their lack of skill

If the master knows their own heart
In simple purity, them we'll serve
As we see the pattern set
We'll all follow with great verve

In the continuing unfolding
Of the bad things into good
But then as normality fades
Revealed is what's now understood

A gentle hand to guide us
Not an imposition from on high
Will see us through the bad times
And end the tears we cry

LIX - VIRTUE

Showing kindness and love
Being one who cares
Prepares you for leadership
Leadership that dares
To show compassion
To see through humanity
And be one who does much good
And sets the people free

Being willing to sacrifice
And thinking of the needs of many
Will make you ready to serve
In a way that shares the plenty
The impossible is the truth
I'm possible! It's clear
No limits really exist
There's nothing we should fear

Vision needs no power grab
Or laws that impose the will
Of lesser beings on the rest of us
Which is the bitterest pill
Freedom cries from within
Virtue has prepared
The leadership we need
To stop us being ensnared

LX - STOPPING EVIL IN ITS TRACKS

Give no power to evil
Stop it in its tracks
Show kindness when confronted
There's no joy in fighting back

An eye for an eye
Will make the whole world blind
So, by not reacting
To yourself, you're being kind

Take the wind from out it's sails
Let evil face itself
Put retribution to one side
It takes two to fight

With no oxygen
The fire soon burns out
So, in this world let freedom
Peace and love, be your only shout

When stopping evil in its tracks
All you need to do
Is try to understand
The evil that men do

For many act in pain
They get angry when they're wronged
So, with compassion and perception
We'll know, we all belong

LXI - BE OF THE LOWLANDS

Be of the lowlands
Not haughty and proud
Be one receiving
One accepting the now

Everything finds its level
Vast rivers flow forth
Into the delta
There we find what they're worth

No matter where you are
In this life where you're found
Make sure you plant your feet
Firmly in the ground

For mountains can fall
And cities can too
Best to stay humble
Whatever you do

For the low places with be exalted
Each dog has it's day
You can win by stooping
Quietness is THE WAY

Be of the lowlands
Not haughty and proud
Be one receiving
One accepting the now

LXII - THE TREASURE HOUSE WITHIN

Close the door
Come inside
See yourself
As an expression
Of light

Let the darkness
Of the selfish you
Fall away
See the ego's falseness
For what it is

The treasures you contain
Far outweigh
The I, the me, the mine
Of unconscious thinking
In reality, you shine

It's time to see
The bright, unblemished you
Time to be, born again
From above
Go back to your Source

I will meet you there
For we are the same
Cast away your wickedness
As I will mine
For we are of the light

LXIII - ONE THING AT A TIME

Do it all in a moment
In smallness achieve all things
The fruit is chewed up, then swallowed
One bite at a time

Work on what's before you
And greatness will be yours
Don't have high expectations
But be conscious in the now

For you to overcome
To be the master of your life
Concentrate on what you're doing
Not on what's to come

What once was complicated
Seems simple as it's done
In the smallness of your actions
Complete everything today

Do what you can do right now
And the mountain will be moved
Confront your difficulties
With quiet simplicity

By doing almost nothing
In a determined way
The trickle of a stream
Cuts through the hardest rocks

LXIV - DILIGENTLY FOLLOW THE PATH

The place of power
The time to effect destiny
Is now

Your life and mine
Is made or broken
In this very moment

Where there is no movement
Observe
Then show THE WAY

Where potential exists
Prevention is the cure
Of what should not be

Keep your life in order
Make sure things
Will move your way

The gentlest of touches
Prevent great heartache
And injury

Give care at the beginning
In the middle and the end
Let the ten thousand things be

Don't resist or grasp
You will not lose
If you seek the achievable

Look into your heart
Listen to your intuition
Show diligence and be fulfilled

LXV - LIGHTLY ROW

When you know
That you don't know
It is easier to listen to your heart
To use your brain
And dance in the rain

To be a guide
To help people decide
THE WAY to go
Just let them flow
Lightly row

Subterfuge
And cunning
Makes people concerned
Be open handed
Don't play tricks

Good fortune follows
Those who swallow
Their own pride

Let others live
And decide how
To live their own lives

LXVI - THE SERVANT KING

To be exalted, lay low
To be appreciated
Humble yourself
To be a leader
Follow your heart
Not your ego

Those who don't seek followers
Will be heeded
Those who wish to be great
Lie low
Those who serve
Are truly royal
And deserve loyalty

In accepting the thoughts
And hearts of others
You yourself are filled
With wisdom from
The tallest mountains
To the deepness
Of what is

Humility lays low enough
To receive all perceptions
Known by sages wise
So, be a servant king
Lead the people through
The darkness they face
And share with them the truth

LXVII - LISTEN TO YOUR HEART

THE WAY to live is clearly shown
THE WAY is able to be known
It's written within your heart
As your consciousness has grown

There is a way that seems right
But its end is in destruction
Look within, if you want to win
For the divine skills we must hone

Mercy and compassion
Loving kindness, charity
Is THE WAY to interact
With others, don't you see

Simplicity, economy
Moderation, thrift
When these are employed
Your life is then a gift

By trying not to be out front
Not seeking to always win
Is an invitation to life
To let humility begin

To raise you up
Like the valleys once made low
For mercy, moderation, being humble
Are THE WAY to go

Let consciousness, be your guide
Listen to your heart

For then you'll know THE WAY
A new life you can start

LXVIII - NON-CONTENDING

Harnessing the talents of others
Is found in listening to
What they'd like to do
Attempting to impose your will
Leads to violence
Try instead to woo

For an army should protect not harm
Anger is not the place to be
When defending fellow countrymen
This is the lasting truth
That's plain to see

To serve and not to impose
To listen rather than to contend
Is THE WAY to keep the peace
Amongst the lives of those
We would seek to mend

Listen out for unity
What do most people desire
And if you posses the power
To change the outcome
Please don't lead us to the fire

LXIX - COMPASSIONATE CONFLICT

The inward look can falter
But when you lift your eyes
You can, if only for a moment
See the connection up on high

A place beyond the ego
Where I and the enemy can't exist
Where both are caught together
Both between and betwixt

For there's a truth resounding
That all are of THE TAO
We belong together
No one needs to bow

An adversary is not an enemy
But one who holds a different view
In a world of opposites
There's someone who's not like you

A battle with soldiers fighting
Where anger is displayed
Is a place for tears and mourning
For the whole human race

So, don't ever make the first move
Meet opponents on life's battlefields
As one who's there to bring peace
And willing to hang up swords and shields

LXX - SIMPLICITY

For now, this eternal moment
You are one of the ten thousand things
And you are meant ... Just to be
Simplicity

The challenge is, the world is material
You are physical, a sensory being
And yet there's a choice, how to live
Choose simplicity

Treasures on the inside
Are more valuable than external ones
It's sad people can't see
How wonderful, is ... simplicity

Nothing to fight for, no enemies
At peace, not wanting anything
Just to live, just to be
Simplicity

LXXI - A HEALTHY LIFE

To be aware of your unawareness
To know that you don't know
To see the difference between
Perceived knowledge
What you know as the unknown
\what you don't know, you don't know
That gives you true strength!

Those without these distinctions are sick
But when we are sick of not knowing
When we want to understand
Our own unawareness
Then we will be enlightened and made whole

Dis-ease ends
When you are sick of being sick
Then all will be revealed to you
And this will bring you to full health
In mind, body, and spirit

LXXII - NO NEED

How tiny, how small
How insignificant we are
When we consider
The vastness of space
And how our place
In it all is
So tiny and so small

Nature majestic, with hurricanes
And the depth of the sea
The mountains so high
Then there's you and me
The forest glade beckons
Sunrise at the beach
The earthquake, the darkness
All have much to teach

Yet the treasures within
Consciousness we are
Outshine the brightness
Of the largest of the stars
The universe is harmony
For we are all one
Each man and woman
Born under the sun

No need to brag
No need to despair
No need to weary
Or your life to compare
Be at peace for
Your life is your own

You belong here
Your purpose will be known
LXXIII - HEAVEN'S NET

As Mother Nature illustrates
To everything there's a season
Patience brings the inevitability
Of good over evil
Of Spring over Fall
Life goes on

There is a plan
Seasons come and go
But progress is inevitable
God sits in the heavens and he laughs
For the plans of the divine
Will always come to pass

There is but one outcome
Be at peace
What may seem like a lost cause
Cannot be stopped
Nay sayers do not know
Nothing escapes heaven's net

LXXIV - NO FEAR!

Melting into the oneness
Like a snowflake beautiful
Solid, liquid, vapour
Just like me and you

A day ahead when you and I
Will be just quiet dust
Our summers nimble mansion gone
And leave humanity without fuss

Imagine then the day
When you have breathed your last
The world goes by without you
And this life for you is past

Die to your ego and
Let your desires leave
Rise above the earth now
So, you can believe

Have no desire to hold onto
A fading epitaph
Your life of no fear has begun
Now you can smile and laugh

Allow, THE TAO, to decide
When life begins and ends
And without fear, your remaining days
On Earth, you can now spend

LXXV - INTRUDER ALERT

Authority given or won
Is there to bless each and everyone
To serve should be your aim
Anything else, is a loser's game

Remember the law of love
Don't make life for others tough
That's not how it's meant to be
"Pharaoh, set my people free!"

By whatever power you have
Enlighten another's path
Lift the burdens of the poor
Don't blame them, that's for sure

If you enhance another's spirit
The world, something beautiful inherits
Don't be taxing people's patience
Be a blessing, not a rain check

Presidents, senators, representatives
Governors, mayors, be sensitive
Don't you lord it over me
I came here to live a life that's free

As for you and I please wake up
It's time to fill up our own cup
And then with a smiling face
Help the whole human race

LXXVI - BE SOFT!

Be the willow, be soft-hearted
Speak soft as those around you, rise
With gentleness approach your life
Tenderness never dies

Don't die within, or criticise
Or with harshness speak
Be ready to accept what comes
And turn the other cheek

Unbroken may your spirit be
In such beauty shine
In this way we'll have the earth
In meekness, it's yours and mine

LXXVII - THE MASTER

Who is clever
The rich man who becomes richer
Or the rich man who shares his wealth ...
The master follows the way of heaven

For heaven balances out
Day with night, storm with calm
Joy with sadness, blessings with grief
No one is overwhelmed by heaven

He sends his sun to shine
On the righteous and the unrighteous
Error is followed by perfection
Patience ... all things must pass

The hoarder and the grasper
Will lose it all, even their soul
But the one who lives well, the master
Will use their wealth for good

Remember, the meek inherit the earth
Poverty will end, heaven blessed are them
So, in your life and mine
Let THE WAY of heaven shine

LXXVIII - THE GREATEST PARADOX

Like the might of the Colorado
Treat your world as porous rock
By being soft and flowing
The powers that be, you'll mock
For if you go through openings
That fall easily into your path
Without much force you will prevail
Where once you found great wrath

In easiness you'll vanquish
By softness and good grace
More than the one who demands
Life must change at a faster pace
When met with an opposing view
Say with interest I don't know
Please explain your point of view
Like it's something you must know

The greatest paradox
That has shown itself to me
Is that in weakness we are strong
That strength is the wrong key
For opening up the world
Serenity and peace within
Will help you get ahead
And all else is a sin

LXXIX - RETURNING INJURY WITH KINDNESS

Quarrelling
Bitterness
Resentment
Inescapable hostility
How can these two sides
Ever be reconciled

Who will be the bigger person
The one who
Returns injury with kindness

However deep our divisions
We are opponents not enemies
We are human
We belong

So, give, without expecting gratitude
The virtuous always find a way to give
To open their hearts
And from their fullness
Give to those empty of love

LXXX - HEARTH AND HOME

An Andalusian shepherd boy once found
That where he was from, was his holy ground
In an old-fashioned feeling, and it's fully grown
Simplicity and peace are always found at home

The swords, now ploughshares in that place
People of the soil, know no disgrace
They live each moment of each day
With love in their hearts, till they pass away

Small shelters only, from the wind and rain
Healthy food they eat, it them sustains
Their clothes do not show off finery
Content, accepting what is, and what they see

No nosey neighbours, are found here
They're happy to help, yet they don't stare
Living their own lives with those near and dear
For these kind folks not even death they fear

Are you content with hearth and home
Or are you striving, contriving, cold as stone
Maybe you should consider a life like these
Who've found a way to live full and free

LXXXI - THE WORLD OF NO THING

From the world of ten thousand things
You will one day leave
You will have to give back
All that you've received

So, open up your heart
Let the ten thousand things flow through
Do not be attached to them
But to THE TAO be true

Put away your cleverness
Bewildered you can be
Don't argue, live with virtue
And you'll be forever free

Don't accumulate
Be a giver from your store
You can't outgive THE TAO
From its plenty you'll get more

Do good to everyone you can
Be generous, just like heaven
Don't be in opposition, and
From evil be you spared

Enter into the world of no thing
Be lighter than the air
And in sweetness you will live your days
And never will you despair

CONCLUSION - NERVOUS ENERGY

Be self-aware, not self conscious
Be confidant in who you are
Let your nervous energy dissipate
See yourself from afar

You are divinity wrapped in humanity
You belong right here
The universe exists within you
There's nothing you should fear

There's never been another
Person just like you
You are an expression of creation
Without you, nothing's true

So be at peace, centre yourself
Be grounded that is all
Take a deep breath and smile
You're never going to fall

You're in the place you're meant to be
As life unfolds right now
Let fear be gone, know yourself
Listen to THE TAO

Be self-assured, express yourself
In your own certainty
Harness the excitement
Use your nervous energy

BARNABAS ENGLAND – REFLECTIONS OF THE TAO – BACKWORD

This book contains the author's reflections of "The TAO TE CHING" by Lao Tzu, the second most purchased book in the world. It is the source document for Taoism and Chinese Buddhism, which the author claims to know very little about.

So, what you have here is a Western mind considering an Eastern text and reflecting on the wisdom found there and then expressed within the context of the author's own life experiences and understandings.

THE TAO translates into the English words THE WAY. THE TAO contains a deep understanding of the nature of reality and the universe, it will give to those who read it and put its wisdom into practice, a better life than they have experienced before.

It was written as advice to leaders and wisdom-based leadership is surely needed in the world today. Maybe this book can help you to take your place amongst those who are called to serve as leaders; however humble that leadership role might be?

Barnabas England is a wellbeing poet, inspirational life coach and public speaker. He is a founder member of the online Community Vision Platform https://waychi.me please do come and join "The Way" and connect with the author there. See also https://the-way.me

Barnabas is also founder and sole editor of the 15,000 strong Facebook group "Be Inspired!" and the Facebook page "Love Revolution" You can email him at 57perception@gmail.com or eventually via his new website: https://barnabasengland.uk

Printed in Great Britain
by Amazon

40263723R00059